Serge Panine, Volume 4

Georges Ohnet

BOOK 4.

CHAPTER XVIII

THE UNIVERSAL CREDIT COMPANY

The banking-house of Cayrol had not a very imposing appearance. It was a narrow two-storied building, the front blackened by time. There was a carriage gateway, on the right-hand side of which was the entrance to the offices. The stairs leading to the first floor were covered by a well- worn carpet. Here was a long corridor into which the different offices opened. On their glass doors might be read: "Payments of dividends. " "Accounts. " "Foreign correspondence. " "General office. " Cayrol's own room was quite at the end, and communicated with his private apartments. Everything breathed of simplicity and honesty. Cayrol had never tried to throw dust into people's eyes. He had started modestly when opening the bank; his business had increased, but his habits had remained the same. It was not a difficult matter to obtain an interview, even by people not known to him. They sent in their cards, and were admitted to his sanctum.

It was amid the coming and going of customers and clerks that Prince Panine came the following day to find Cayrol. For the first time Serge had put himself out for the banker. He was introduced with marks of the most profound respect. The great name of Desvarennes seemed to cast a kind of halo round his head in the eyes of the clerks.

Cayrol, a little embarrassed, but still resolute, went toward him. Serge seemed nervous and somewhat abrupt in manner. He foresaw some difficulty.

"Well! my dear fellow, " he said, without sitting down. "What are you up to? I have waited since yesterday for the money you promised me. "

Cayrol scratched his ear, and felt taken aback by this plain speaking.

"The fact is—" stammered he.

"Have you forgotten your engagement? " asked Serge, frowning.

1

"No, " replied Cayrol, speaking slowly, "but I met Madame Desvarennes yesterday. "

"And what had that to do with your intentions? "

"Zounds! It had everything to do with them. Your mother-in-law made a scene, and forbade my lending you any money. You must understand, my dear Prince, that my relations with Madame Desvarennes are important. I hold a great deal of money of hers in my bank. She first gave me a start. I cannot, without appearing ungrateful, act contrary to her will. Place yourself in my position, and judge impartially of the terrible alternative between obliging you and displeasing my benefactress. "

"Don't cry; it is useless, " said Serge, with a scornful laugh. "I sympathize with your troubles. You side with the money-bags. It remains to be seen whether you will gain by it. "

"My dear Prince, I swear to you that I am in despair, " cried Cayrol, annoyed at the turn the interview was taking. "Listen; be reasonable! I don't know what you have done to your mother-in-law, but she seems much vexed with you. In your place I would rather make a few advances than remain hostile toward Madame Desvarennes. That would mend matters, you see. Flies are not to be caught with vinegar. "

Serge looked contemptuously at Cayrol, and put on his hat with supreme insolence.

"Pardon me, my dear fellow; as a banker you are excellent when you have any money to spare, but as a moralist you are highly ridiculous. "

And, turning on his heel, he quitted the office, leaving Cayrol quite abashed. He passed along the corridor switching his cane with suppressed rage. Madame Desvarennes had, with one word, dried up the source from which he had been drawing most of the money which he had spent during the last three months. He had to pay a large sum that evening at the club, and he did not care to apply to the money-lenders of Paris.

He went down the stairs wondering how he would get out of this scrape! Go to Madame Desvarennes and humble himself as Cayrol advised? Never! He regretted, for a moment, the follies which had led him into this difficulty. He ought to have been able to live on two hundred thousand francs a year! He had squandered money foolishly, and now the inexhaustible well from which he had drawn his treasure was closed by an invincible will.

He was crossing the gateway, when a well-known voice struck his ear, and he turned round. Herzog, smiling in his enigmatical manner, was before him. Serge bowed, and wanted to pass on, but the financier put his hand on his arm, saying:

"What a hurry you are in, Prince. I suppose your pocketbook is full of notes, and you are afraid of being plundered. "

And with his finger, Herzog touched the silver mounted pocketbook, the corner of which was peeping out of the Prince's pocket. Panine could not control a gesture of vexation, which made the financier smile.

"Am I wrong? " asked Herzog. "Can our friend Cayrol have refused your request? By-the-bye, did you not quarrel with Madame Desvarennes yesterday? Whoever was it told me that? Your mother-in-law spoke of cutting off all your credit, and from your downcast look I guess that fool Cayrol has obeyed the orders he has received. "

Serge, exasperated and stamping with rage, wanted to speak, but it was no easy matter interrupting Herzog. Besides, there was something in the latter's look which annoyed Serge. His glance seemed to be fathoming the depths of Panine's pockets, and the latter instinctively tightened his arms across his chest, so that Herzog might not see that his pocketbook was empty.

"What are you talking about? " asked Serge, at last, with a constrained smile.

"About things which must greatly interest you, " said Herzog, familiarly. "Come, be sincere. Cayrol has just refused you a sum of money. He's a simpleton! How much do you want? Will a hundred thousand francs do just now? "

And writing a few words on a check, the financier handed it to Serge, adding:

"A man of your position should not be in any difficulty for such a paltry sum! "

"But, sir, " said Serge, astonished, and pushing away Herzog's hand.

"Accept it, and don't feel indebted to me. It is hardly worth while between you and me. "

And taking Panine's arm Herzog walked on with him.

"Your carriage is there? all right, mine will follow. I want to talk to you. Your troubles cannot last. I will show you the means of extricating yourself and that without delay, my dear sir. "

And without consulting Panine he seated himself beside him in the carriage.

"I told you once, if you remember, " continued the financier, "that I might prove useful to you. You were haughty, and I did not insist; yet you see the day has come. Let me speak frankly with you. It is my usual manner, and there is some good in it. "

"Speak, " answered Serge, rather puzzled.

"You find yourself at this moment, vulgarly speaking, left in the lurch. Your wants are many and your resources few. "

"At least—" protested Serge.

"Good! There you are refractory, " said the financier, laughingly, "and I have not finished. The day after your marriage you formed your household on a lavish footing; you gave splendid receptions; you bought race- horses; in short, you went the pace like a great lord. Undoubtedly it costs a lot of money to keep up such an establishment. As you spent without counting the cost, you confounded the capital with the interest, so that at this moment you are three parts ruined. I don't think you would care to change your mode of living, and it is too late in the day to cut down expenses and exist on what remains? No. Well, to keep up your present style you need at least a million francs every year. "

"You calculate like Cocker, " remarked Serge, smiling with some constraint.

"That is my business, " answered Herzog. "There are two ways by which you can obtain that million. The first is by making it up with your mother- in-law, and consenting, for money, to live under her dominion. I know her, she will agree to this. "

"But, " said Serge, "I refuse to submit. "

"In that case you must get out of your difficulties alone. "

"And how? " inquired the Prince, with astonishment.

Herzog looked at him seriously.

"By entering on the path which I am ready to open up to you, " replied Herzog, "and in which I will guide you. By going in for business. "

Serge returned Herzog's glance and tried to read his face, but found him impenetrable.

"To go into business one needs experience, and I have none. "

"Mine will suffice, " retorted the financier.

"Or money, " continued the Prince, " and I have none, either. "

"I don't ask money from you. I offer you some. "

"What, then, do I bring into the concern? "

"The prestige of your name, and your relations with Madame Desvarennes. "

The Prince answered, haughtily:

"My relations are personal, and I doubt whether they will serve you. My mother-in-law is hostile, and will do nothing for me. As to my name, it does not belong to me, it belongs to those who bore it nobly before me. "

"Your relations will serve me, " said Herzog. "I am satisfied. Your mother-in-law cannot get out of your being her daughter's husband, and for that you are worth your weight in gold. As to your name, it is just because it has been nobly borne that it is valuable. Thank your ancestors, therefore, and make the best of the only heritage they left you. Besides, if you care to examine things closely, your ancestors will not have reason to tremble in their graves. What did they do formerly? They imposed taxes on their vassals and extorted money from the vanquished. We financiers do the same. Our vanquished are the speculators; our vassals the shareholders. And what a superiority there is about our proceedings! There is no violence. We persuade; we fascinate; and the money flows into our coffers. What do I say? They beseech us to take it. We reign without contest. We are princes, too princes of finance. We have founded an aristocracy as proud and as powerful as the old one. Feudality of nobility no longer exists; it has given way to that of money. "

Serge laughed. He saw what Herzog was driving at.

"Your great barons of finance are sometimes subject to executions, " said he.

"Were not Chalais, Cinq-Mars, Biron, and Montmorency executed? " asked Herzog, with irony.

"That was on a scaffold, " replied Panine.

"Well! the speculator's scaffold is the Bourse! But only small dabblers in money succumb; the great ones are safe from danger. They are supported in their undertakings by such powerful and numerous interests that they cannot fail without involving public credit; even governments are forced to come to their aid. One of these powerful and indestructible enterprises I have dreamed of grafting on to the European Credit Company, the Universal Credit Company. Its very name is a programme in itself. To stretch over the four quarters of the globe like an immense net, and draw into its meshes all financial speculators: such is its aim. Nobody will be able to withstand us. I am offering you great things, but I dream of still greater. I have ideas. You will see them developed, and will profit by them, if you join my fortunes. You are ambitious, Prince. I guessed it; but your ambition hitherto has been satisfied with small things — luxurious indulgences and triumphs of elegance! What are these worth to what I can give you? The sphere in which you move is narrow. I will make it immense. You will no longer reign over a small social circle, you will rule a world. "

Serge, more affected than he cared to show, tried to banter.

"Are you repeating the prologue to Faust? " asked he. "Where is your magical compact? Must I sign it? "

"Not at all. Your consent is sufficient. Look into the business, study it at your leisure, and measure the results; and then if it suit you, you can sign a deed of partnership. Then in a few years you may possess a fortune surpassing all that you have dreamed of. "

The financier remained silent. Serge was weighing the question. Herzog was happy; he had shown himself to all Paris in company with Madame Desvarennes's son-in-law. He had already realized one of his projects. The carriage was just passing down the Champs Elysees. The weather was lovely, and in the distance could be seen the trees of the Tuileries and the different monuments of the Place de la Concorde bathed in blue mist. Groups of horsemen were cantering along the side avenues. Long files of carriages were rolling rapidly by with well-dressed ladies. The capital displayed at that hour all the splendor of its luxury. It was Paris in all its strength and gayety.

Herzog stretched out his hand, and calling the Prince's attention to the sight, said:

"There's your empire! "

Then, looking at him earnestly, he asked:

"Is it agreed? "

Serge hesitated for a moment, and then bowed his head, saying:

"It is agreed. "

Herzog pulled the check-string communicating with the coachman and alighted.

"Good-by, " said he to Panine.

He slipped into his own carriage, which had followed closely behind, and drove off.

From that day, even Jeanne had a rival. The fever of speculation had seized on Serge; he had placed his little finger within the wheels and he must follow—body, name, and soul. The power which this new game exercised over him was incredible. It was quite different to the stupid games at the club, always the same. On the Bourse, everything was new, unexpected, sudden, and formidable. The intensity of the feelings were increased a hundredfold, owing to the importance of the sums risked.

It was really a splendid sight to see Herzog manipulating matters, maneuvering with a miraculous dexterity millions of francs. And then the field for operations was large. Politics, the interests of nations, were the mainsprings which impelled the play, and the game assumed diplomatic vastness and financial grandeur.

From his private office Herzog issued orders, and whether his ability was really extraordinary, or whether fortune exceptionally favored him, success was certain. Serge, from the first week, realized considerable sums. This brilliant success threw him in a state of great excitement. He believed everything that Herzog said to him as if it were gospel. He saw the world bending under the yoke which he was about to impose upon it. People working and toiling every day were doing so for him alone, and like one of those kings who had conquered the world, he pictured all the treasures of the earth laid at his feet. From that time he lost the sense of right and wrong. He admitted the unlikely, and found the impossible quite natural. He was a docile tool in the hands of Herzog.

The rumor of this unforeseen change in Panine's circumstances soon reached Madame Desvarennes's ears. The mistress was frightened, and sent for Cayrol, begging him to remain a director of the European Credit, in order to watch the progress of the new affair. With her practical common sense, she foresaw disasters, and even regretted that Serge had not confined himself to cards and reckless living.

Cayrol was most uneasy, and made a confidant of his wife, who, deeply troubled, told Panine the fears his friends entertained on his account. The Prince smiled disdainfully, saying these fears were the effect of plebeian timidity. The mistress understood nothing of great speculations, and Cayrol was a narrow-minded banker! He knew what he was doing. The results of his speculations were mathematical. So far they had not disappointed his hopes. The great

Universal Credit Company, of which he was going to be a director, would bring him in such an immense fortune that he would be independent of Madame Desvarennes.

Jeanne, terrified at this blind confidence, tried to persuade him. Serge took her in his arms, kissed her, and banished her fears.

Madame Desvarennes had forbidden her people to tell Micheline anything of what was going on, as she wished her to remain in perfect ignorance. By a word, the mistress, if she could not have prevented the follies of which Serge was guilty, could, at least, have spared herself and her daughter. It would have only been necessary to reveal his behavior and betrayal to Micheline, and to provoke a separation. If the house of Desvarennes were no longer security for Panine, his credit would fall. Disowned by his mother-in-law, and publicly given up by her, he would be of no use to Herzog, and would be promptly thrown over by him. The mistress did not wish her daughter to know the heartrending truth. She would not willingly cause her to shed tears, and therefore preferred risking ruin.

Micheline, too, tried to hide her troubles from her mother. She knew too well that Serge would have the worst of it if he got into her black books. With the incredible persistence of a loving heart, she hoped to win back Serge. Thus a terrible misunderstanding caused these two women to remain inactive and silent, when, by united efforts, they might, perhaps, have prevented dangers.

The great speculation was already being talked about. Herzog was boldly placing his foot on the summit whereon the five or six demigods, who ruled the stock market, were firmly placed. The audacious encroachments of this newcomer had vexed these formidable potentates, and already they had decided secretly his downfall because he would not let them share in his profits.

One morning, the Parisians, on awakening, found the walls placarded with notices advertising the issue of shares in the Universal Credit Company, and announcing the names of the directors, among which appeared that of the Prince. Some were members of the Legion d'Honneur; others recent members of the Cabinet Council, and Prefets retired into private life. A list of names to dazzle the public, but all having a weak point.

This created a great sensation in the business world. Madame Desvarennes's son-in-law was on the board. It was a good speculation, then? People consulted the mistress, who found herself somewhat in a dilemma; either she must disown her son-in-law, or speak well of the affair. Still she did not hesitate, for she was loyal and honest above all things. She declared the speculation was a poor one, and did all she could to prevent any of her friends becoming shareholders.

The issue of shares was disastrous. The great banks remained hostile, and capitalists were mistrustful. Herzog landed a few million francs. Doorkeepers and cooks brought him their savings. He covered expenses. But it was no use advertising and puffing in the newspapers, as a word had gone forth which paralyzed the speculation. Ugly rumors were afloat. Herzog's German origin was made use of by the bankers, who whispered that the aim of the Universal Credit Company was exclusively political. It was to establish branch banks in every part of the world to further the interests of German industry. Further, at a given moment, Germany might have need of a loan in case of war, and the Universal Credit Company would be there to supply the necessary aid to the great military nation.

Herzog was not a man to be put down without resisting, and he made supreme efforts to float his undertaking. He caused a number of unissued shares to be sold on 'Change, and had them bought up by his own men, thus creating a fictitious interest in the company. In a few days the shares rose and were at a premium, simply through the jobbery to which Herzog lent himself.

Panine was little disposed to seek for explanations, and, besides, had such unbounded faith in his partner that he suspected nothing. He remained in perfect tranquillity. He had increased his expenditure, and his household was on a royal footing. Micheline's sweetness emboldened him; he no longer took the trouble of dissimulating, and treated his young wife with perfect indifference.

Jeanne and Serge met every day at the little house in the Avenue Maillot. Cayrol was too much engaged with the new anxieties which Herzog caused him, to look after his wife, and left her quite free to amuse herself. Besides, he had not the least suspicion. Jeanne, like all guilty women, overwhelmed him with kind attentions, which the good man mistook for proofs of love. The fatal passion was growing daily stronger in the young woman's heart, and she would have found it impossible to have given up her dishonorable happiness with Panine. She felt herself capable of doing anything to preserve her lover.

Jeanne had already said, "Oh! if we were but free! " And they formed projects. They would go away to Lake Lugano, and, in a villa hidden by trees and shrubs, would enjoy the pleasures of being indissolubly united. The woman was more eager than the man in giving way to these visions of happiness. She sometimes said, "What hinders us now? Let us go. " But Serge, prudent and discreet, even in the most affectionate moments, led Jeanne to take a more sensible view. What was the use of a scandal? Did they not belong to each other?

Then the young woman reproached him for not loving her as much as she loved him. She was tired of dissimulating; her husband was an object of horror to her, and she had to tell him untruths and submit to his caresses which were revolting to her. Serge calmed her with a kiss, and bade her wait awhile.

Pierre, rendered anxious on hearing that Serge had joined Herzog in his dangerous financial speculations, had left his mines and had just arrived. The letters which Micheline addressed to the friend of her youth, her enforced confidant in trouble, were calm and resigned. Full of pride, she had carefully hidden from Pierre the cause of her troubles. He was the last person by whom she would like to be pitied, and her letters had represented Serge as repentant and full of good feeling. Marechal, for similar reasons, had kept his friend in the dark. He feared Pierre's interference, and he wished to spare Madame Desvarennes the grief of seeing her adopted son quarreling with her son-in-law.

But the placards announcing the establishment of the Universal Credit Company made their way into the provinces, and one morning Pierre found some stuck on the walls of his establishment. Seeing the name of Panine, and not that of Cayrol, Pierre shuddered. The unpleasant ideas which he experienced formerly when Herzog was introduced to the Desvarennes recurred to his mind. He wrote to the mistress to ask what was going on, and not receiving an answer, he started off without hesitation for Paris.

He found Madame Desvarennes in a terrible state of excitement. The shares had just fallen a hundred and twenty francs. A panic had ensued. The affair was considered as absolutely lost, and the shareholders were aggravating matters by wanting to sell out at once.

Savinien was just coming away from the mistress's room. He wanted to see the downfall of the Prince, whom he had always hated, looking upon him as a usurper of his own rights upon the fortune of the Desvarennes. He began lamenting to his aunt, when she turned upon him with unusual harshness, and he felt bound as he said, laughing, to leave the "funereal mansion. "

Cayrol, as much interested in the affairs of the Prince as if they were his own, went backward and forward between the Rue Saint-Dominique and the Rue Taitbout, pale and troubled, but without losing his head. He had already saved the European Credit Company by separating it six weeks before from the Universal Credit Company, notwithstanding Madame Desvarennes's supplications to keep them together, in the hope that the one would save the other. But Cayrol, practical, clear, and implacable, had refused, for the first time, to obey Madame Desvarennes. He acted with the resolution of a captain of a vessel, who throws overboard a portion of the cargo to save the ship, the crew, and the rest of the merchandise. He did well, and the European Credit was safe. The shares had fallen a little, but a favorable reaction was already showing itself. The name of Cayrol, and his presence at the head of affairs, had reassured the public, and the shareholders gathered round him, passing a vote of confidence.

The banker, devoted to his task, next sought to save Panine, who was at that very moment robbing him of his honor and happiness in the house of the Avenue Maillot.

Pierre, Cayrol, and Madame Desvarennes met in Marechal's private office. Pierre declared that it was imperative to take strong measures and to speak to the Prince. It was the duty of the mistress to enlighten Panine, who was no doubt Herzog's dupe.

Madame Desvarennes shook her head sadly. She feared that Serge was not a dupe but an accomplice. And what could she tell him? Let him ruin himself! He would not believe her. She knew how he received her advice and bore her remonstrances.

An explanation between her and Serge was impossible, and her interference would only hurry him into the abyss.

"Well, then, I will speak to him, " said Pierre, resolutely.

"No, " said Madame Desvarennes, "not you! Only one here can tell him efficaciously what he must hear, and that is Cayrol. Let us above all things keep guard over our words and our behavior. On no account must Micheline suspect anything. "

Thus, at the most solemn moments, when fortune and honor, perhaps, were compromised, the mother thought of her daughter's welfare and happiness.

Cayrol went up to the Prince's rooms. He had just come in, and was opening his letters, while having a cigarette in the smoking-room. A door, covered by curtains, led to a back stair which opened into the courtyard. Cayrol had gone up that way, feeling sure that by so doing he would not meet Micheline.

On seeing Jeanne's husband, Serge rose quickly. He feared that Cayrol had discovered everything, and instinctively stepped backward. The banker's manner soon undeceived him. He was serious, but not in a rage. He had evidently come on business.

"Well, my dear Cayrol, " said the Prince, gayly, "what good fortune has brought you here? "

"If it is fortune, it is certainly not good fortune, " answered the banker, gravely. "I wish to have some talk with you, and I shall be grateful if you will listen patiently. "

"Oh! oh! " said Serge. "How serious you are. You have some heavy payments on hand, and want a little help, eh? I will speak to Herzog. "

Cayrol looked at the Prince in amazement. So he did not suspect anything? Such carelessness and negligence frightened him. The banker resolved to proceed clearly, and without beating about the bush; to do away with such blind confidence a thunderbolt was necessary.

"I have not come about my business, but yours, " returned Cayrol. "The Universal Credit Company is on the eve of disaster; there is still time for you to withdraw safely and soundly from the sinking wreck. I bring you the means. "

Serge laughed.

"Thank you, Cayrol; you are very kind, my friend. I know your intentions are good, but I don't believe a word you are saying. You have come from Madame Desvarennes. You are both agreed that I shall give up the Universal Credit, but I will not yield to any pressure. I know what I am doing. Be easy. "

And quietly lighting another cigarette, he gracefully puffed the smoke toward the ceiling. Cayrol did not trouble to argue, but took a newspaper from his pocket and handed it to Panine, simply saying, "Read! "

It was an article in a reliable financial paper prophesying the failure of the Universal Credit Company, and basing its statements on irrefutable calculations. Serge took the paper and looked over it. He turned pale and crushed it in his hand.

"What infamy! " cried he. "I know our adversaries are enraged. Yes, they know that our new company is destined to crush them in the future, and they are doing all they can to run us aground. Jealousy! Envy! There is no other foundation for these rumors, and they are unworthy a serious man's attention. "

"There is neither envy nor jealousy. All is true, " said Cayrol. "You will admit that I am your sincere friend? Well, I swear to you that the situation is terrible, and you must resign your directorship of the Universal Credit without loss of time. There's not a moment to lose. Sit down and write your resignation. "

"Do you think I am a child to be led by the nose like that? " asked the Prince, in a passion. "If you are sincere, Cayrol, as I wish to believe, I also think you are a fool. You don't understand! As to drawing out of the company, never! I have a lot of money invested in it. "

"Well, lose your money, Madame Desvarennes will pay you back. At least you can save your name. "

"Ah, I see you are conniving with her! " exclaimed the Prince, loudly. "Don't tell me another word, I don't believe you. I shall go straight to the office, and I will speak to Herzog. We will take measures to prosecute the papers for libel if they dare to publish these untruths. "

Cayrol saw that nothing would convince Panine. He hoped that an interview with Herzog would enlighten him. He left the matter to chance, as reasoning was of no avail, and went down to the mistress.

Serge drove to the Universal Credit Company. It was the first day in the new offices. Herzog had furnished them splendidly, thinking that this would give the shareholders a high opinion of the undertaking. How could they have any doubts when they saw such splendid furniture and large offices? How could they refuse to place their money in the hands of speculators that could cover their floors with such soft carpets? The porters, with their dark blue and red cloth liveries, and buttons with the company's monogram on them, answered inquiries with haughty condescension. Everything foretold success. It was in the air. You could hear the cashier shovelling heaps of gold. The people who had placed the Universal Credit Company on such a footing were either very powerful or very impudent.

Serge walked in, as he would have done at home, with his hat on, amid a number of small shareholders, who had come full of anxiety after reading the accounts in the newspapers, and who felt full of confidence after seeing the splendor of the place. Panine reached Herzog's office, but when about to open the door, loud voices struck his ear. The financier was arguing with a director, and Panine listened.

"The speculation is safe and sure, " Herzog was saying. "The shares are low, I know, because I have ceased to keep them up. I have given orders in London, Vienna, and Berlin, and we are buying up all shares that are offered in the market. I shall then run the shares up again, and we shall realize an enormous sum. It is most simple. "

"But it is shady, " said the other voice.

"Why? I defend myself as I am attacked. The great banks seek to deteriorate my stock. I buy in, and take it out of my adversaries. Is it not just and lawful? "

Panine breathed freely and felt reassured. The depreciation was caused by Herzog; he had just said so. There was nothing to fear then. It was just a trick of Herzog's, and the company would come out brighter than ever.

Serge went in.

"Oh! here's Prince Panine, " said Herzog. "Ask him what he thinks of the matter. I defer to his judgment. "

"I don't want to know anything, " said Serge. "I have full confidence in you, my dear manager, and our business will prosper in your hands, I am sure. Besides, I know the manoeuvres of our opponents, and I think every financial means justifiable to answer them. "

"Ah! What did I say to you a few minutes ago? " cried Herzog, addressing his questioner in a tone of triumph. "Let me act and you will see. Besides, I don't want to keep you against your will, " he added, harshly. "You are at liberty to withdraw from us if you like. "

The other protested that what he had said was for the best interests of all concerned. He did not dream of leaving the company; on the contrary, they might rely on him. He appreciated the experience and ability of Herzog too well to separate his fortune from his friend's. And, shaking hands with the financier, he took his leave.

"Come! What is all this clamor in the newspapers? " asked Serge, when he found himself alone with Herzog. "Do you know that the articles published are very perfidious? "

"All the more perfidious because they are founded on truth, " said the financier, coldly.

"What do you mean? " cried Serge, in alarm.

"The truth. Do you think I am to tell you lies as I did to that idiot who has just gone out? The Universal Credit has at this moment a screw loose. But patience! I have an idea, and in a fortnight the shares will have doubled in value. I have a splendid scheme in hand which will kill the gas companies. It is a plan for lighting by magnesium. Its effect will be startling. I shall publish sensational articles describing the invention in the London and Brussels papers. Gas shares will fall very low. I shall buy up all I can, and when I am master of the situation, I shall announce that the threatened gas companies are buying up the invention. Shares will rise again, and I shall realize a goodly sum, which will be for the benefit of the Universal Credit. "

"But for such a formidable speculation foreign agents will require security? "

"I will offer it to them. I have here ten million francs' worth of shares in the European Credit belonging to Cayrol. We will give the cashier a joint receipt for them. The speculation will last three days. It is safe, and when the result is achieved we will replace the shares, and take back the receipt. "

"But, " asked Serge, "is this plan of taking the shares which don't belong to us legal? "

"It is a transfer, " said Herzog, with simplicity. "Besides, don't forget that we have to do with Cayrol, that is to say with a partner. "

"Suppose we tell him of it, " insisted the Prince.

"No! The deuce! We should have to explain everything to him. He knows what's what, and would find the idea too good, and want a share of the spoil. No! Sign that, and don't be alarmed. The sheep will be back in the fold before the shepherd comes to count them. "

A dark presentiment crossed Serge's mind, and he was afraid. At that moment, when his fate was being decided, he hesitated to go deeper into the rut where he had already been walking too long. He stood silent and undecided. Confused thoughts crowded his brain; his temples throbbed, and a buzzing noise sounded in his ears. But the thought of giving up his liberty, and again subjecting himself to Madame Desvarennes's protection was like the lash of a whip, and he blushed for having hesitated.

Herzog looked at him, and, smiling in a constrained way, said:

"You, too, may give up the affair if you like. If I share it with you it is because you are so closely allied to me. I don't so very much care to cut the pear in two. Don't think that I am begging of you to be my partner! Do as you like. "

Serge caught hold of the paper and, having signed it, handed it to the financier.

"All right, " said Herzog. "I shall leave to-night and be absent three days. Watch the money market. You will see the results of my calculations. "

And shaking hands with the Prince, Herzog went to the cashier to get the scrip and deposit the receipt.

CHAPTER XIX

SIN GROWS BOLDER

There was a party at Cayrol's. In the drawing-rooms of the mansion in the Rue Taitbout everything was resplendent with lights, and there was quite a profusion of flowers. Cayrol had thought of postponing the party, but was afraid of rousing anxieties, and like an actor who, though he has just lost his father, must play the following day, so Cayrol gave his party and showed a smiling face, so as to prevent harm to his business.

Matters had taken a turn for the worse during the last three days. The bold stroke, to carry out which Herzog had gone to London so as to be more secret, had been got wind of. The fall of the shares had not taken place. Working with considerable sums of money, the loss on the difference was as great as the gains would have been. The shares belonging to the European Credit Company had defrayed the cost of the game. It was a disaster. Cayrol, in his anxiety, had applied for the scrip and had only found the receipt given to the cashier. Although the transaction was most irregular, Cayrol had not said anything; but, utterly cast down, had gone to Madame Desvarennes to tell her of the fact.

The Prince was in bed, pretending to be ill. His wife, happily ignorant of all that was going on, rejoiced secretly at his indisposition because she was allowed to nurse him and have him all to herself. Panine, alarmed at the check they had experienced, was expecting Herzog with feverish impatience, and to keep out of sight had chosen the privacy of his own room.

Still, Cayrol had been allowed to see him, and with great circumspection told him that his non-appearance at the same time that Herzog was absent was most fatal for the Universal Credit Company. It was absolutely necessary that he should be seen in public. He must come to his party, and appear with a calm face. Serge promised to come, and had imposed on Micheline the heavy task of accompanying him to Jeanne's. It was the first time since her return from Nice that she had entered the house of her husband's mistress.

The concert was over, and a crowd of guests were coming from the large drawing-room to the boudoir and little drawing-room.

"The symphony is over. Ouf! " said Savinien, yawning.

"You don't like music? " asked Marechal, with a laugh.

"Yes, military music. But two hours of Schumann and Mendelssohn at high pressure is too much for one man. But I say, Marechal, what do you think of Mademoiselle Herzog's being at Cayrol's soiree. It is a little too strong. "

"How so? "

"Why, the father has bolted, and the daughter is preparing a dance. Each has a different way of using their feet. "

"Very pretty, Monsieur Desvarennes, but I advise you to keep your flashes of wit to yourself, " said Marechal, seriously. "That may not suit everybody. "

"Oh, Marechal, you, too, making a fuss! "

And turning on his heel, he went to the refreshment table.

Prince and Princess Panine were just coming in. Micheline was smiling, and Serge was pale, though calm. Cayrol and Jeanne came toward them. Everybody turned to look at them. Jeanne, without embarrassment, shook hands with her friend. Cayrol bowed respectfully to Micheline.

"Princess, " he said, "will you honor me by taking my arm? You are just in time, they are going to begin dancing. "

"Not myself, though, thank you, " replied Micheline, with a sad smile, "I am still very weak, but I will look on. "

And on Cayrol's arm she entered the large drawing-room. Serge followed with Jeanne.

The festivities were at their height. The orchestra was playing a waltz, and in a whirl of silk and gauze the young people seemed to be thoroughly enjoying themselves.

Suzanne Herzog was sitting alone near a window, in a simple white dress, and without a single ornament. Marechal had just approached her, and she had welcomed him with a smile.

"Are you not dancing to-night, Mademoiselle? " he asked.

"I am waiting to be invited, " she answered, sadly, "and, like sister Anne, I see nobody coming. There are ugly reports abroad about my father's fortune, and the Argonauts are drawing off. "

"Will you give me a dance? " said Marechal. "I don't dance to perfection, never having practised much, but with a good will. "

"Thank you, Monsieur Marechal, I would rather talk. I am not very cheerful to-night, and, believe me, I only came because Madame Desvarennes wished it. I would rather have remained at home. Business has gone wrong with my father by what I can hear, for I don't know what goes on at the office. I feel more inclined to cry than to laugh. Not that I regret the loss of money, you know; I don't care for it, but my father must be in despair. "

Marechal listened silently to Suzanne, not daring to tell her what he thought of Herzog, and respected the real ignorance or willing blindness of the young girl who did not doubt her father's loyalty.

The Princess, leaning on Cayrol's arm, had just finished promenading round the rooms, when she perceived Suzanne and, leaving the banker, came and seated herself beside her. Many of the guests looked at each other and whispered words which Micheline did not hear, and if she had heard would not have understood. "It is heroic! " some said. Others answered, "It is the height of impudence. "

The Princess was talking with Suzanne and was looking at her husband who, leaning against a door, was following Jeanne with his eyes.

At a sign from Cayrol, Marechal left the room. The secretary joined Madame Desvarennes, who had come with Pierre and had remained in Cayrol's private office. During this party matters of moment were to be discussed, and a consultation was about to take place between the interested parties. On seeing Marechal enter, Madame only uttered one word:

"Cayrol? "

"Here he is, " answered the secretary.

Cayrol came in, hurriedly.

"Well, " he asked, with great anxiety, "have you any news? "

"Pierre has just come from London, " answered the mistress. "What we feared is true. Herzog, conjointly with my son-in-law, has made use of the ten millions belonging to the European Credit. "

"Do you think that Herzog has really bolted? " inquired Marechal.

"No! he is too deep for that, " replied Cayrol. "He will return. He knows that in compromising the Prince it is as if he had compromised the firm of Desvarennes, therefore he is quite easy on the matter. "

"Can the one be saved without the other? " asked the mistress.

"It is impossible. Herzog has so firmly bound up his interests with those of the Prince that it will be necessary to extricate both or let both perish together. "

"Well, we must save Herzog into the bargain, then! " said Madame Desvarennes, coldly. "But by what means? "

"These, " answered Cayrol. "The shares taken away by Herzog, under the security of the Prince's signature, were deposited by the shareholders. When the Universal Credit removed to its new offices, these shares were taken away by mistake. It will suffice to replace the scrip. I will give back the receipt to the Prince and all trace of this deplorable affair will be wiped out. "

"But the numbers of the shares will not be the same, " said Madame Desvarennes, accustomed to minute regularity in all operations.

"We can explain the change by feigning a sale when they were high, and buying them up when low. We will show a profit, and the shareholders will not quarrel. Besides, I reserve the right of divulging Herzog's fraud without implicating Panine, if the shareholders insist. Trust me, I will catch Herzog another time. It is my stupid confidence in that man which has been partly the cause of this disaster. I will make your business mine and force him to shell out. I shall leave for London to- night, by the 1.50 train. Promptness of action in such a case is the first step toward success. "

"Thank you, Cayrol, " said the mistress. "Have my daughter and the Prince arrived? "

"Yes, Serge is calm; he has more power over himself than I could have believed. "

"What does it matter to him what is going on? Is it he who will feel the blow? No. He knows that I shall go on working to keep him in idleness and maintain him in luxury. I may think myself lucky if he is reclaimed by this hard lesson, and does not again begin to rummage in other people's safes, for then I should be unable to save him. "

The mistress rose and, with flashing eyes, walked up and down the room.

"Oh, the wretch! " she said. "If ever my daughter ceases to come between him and me! "

A terrible gesture finished the sentence.

Cayrol, Marechal, and Pierre looked at each other. The same thought came to their minds, dark and fearful. In a paroxysm of rage this fond mother, this energetic and passionate woman, would be capable of killing any one.

"You remember what I told you one day, " murmured Marechal, approaching Cayrol.

"I would prefer the hatred of ten men to that of such a woman, " answered Cayrol.

"Cayrol! " continued Madame Desvarennes, after a few moments of meditation, "the conduct of the business of which you spoke to us a little while ago depends solely on you, does it not? "

"On me alone. "

"Do it at once, then, cost me what it may. Has it been noised abroad? "

"No one has the slightest suspicion. I have not mentioned it to a living soul, " said the banker—"except to my wife, " added he with a frankness which drew a smile from Pierre. "But my wife and I are one. "

"What did she say? " asked Madame Desvarenes, looking straight at Cayrol.

"If I had been the person concerned, " he said, "she could not possibly have been more affected. She loves you so much, Madame, you and those belonging to you. She besought me to do all in my power to get the Prince out of this scrape. She had tears in her eyes: And, truly, if I did not feel bound to serve you from gratitude I would do it for her sake and to give her pleasure. I was touched, I can assure you. Really, she has a heart! "

Marechal exchanged a look with Madame Desvarennes, who advanced toward the banker, and shook him by the hand, saying:

"Cayrol, you are truly a good man! "

"I know it, " said Cayrol, smiling to hide his emotion, "and you may rely upon me. "

Micheline appeared on the threshold of the room. Through the half-open door the dancers could be seen passing to and fro, and the sound of music floated in the air.

"What has become of you, mamma? I hear that you have been here for more than an hour. "

"I was talking on business matters with these gentlemen, " answered Madame Desvarennes, smoothing from her brow the traces of her cares by an effort of will. "But you, dear, how do you feel? Are you not tired? "

"Not more so than usual, " replied Micheline, looking round to follow the movements of her husband, who was trying to reach Jeanne.

"Why did you come to this party? It was unwise. "

"Serge wished me to come, and I did not care to let him come without me. "

"Eh! dear me! " exclaimed Madame Desvarennes. "Let him do what he likes. Men are savages. When you are ill it won't hurt him. "

"I am not ill, and I won't be, " resumed Micheline, warmly. "We are going away now. "

She motioned to Serge with her fan. Panine came to her.

"You will take me home, won't you, Serge? "

"Certainly, dear one, " answered Serge.

Jeanne, who was listening at a distance, raised her hand to her forehead as a sign that she wanted him. A feeling of surprise came over the Prince, and he did not understand what she meant. Micheline had seen the sign. A deadly pallor spread over her features, and a cold perspiration broke out on her forehead. She felt so ill that she could have cried out. It was the first time she had seen Serge and Jeanne together since the dreadful discovery at Nice. She had avoided witnessing their meeting, feeling uncertain of herself, and fearing to lose her self- control. But seeing the two lovers before her, devouring each other with their looks, and making signs to each other, made her feel most terribly jealous and angry.

Serge had decided to obey the imperious signs which Jeanne made to him, and turning toward his wife, said:

"I remember now, my dear, that before going home I must call at the club. I promised, and cannot put it off. Excuse my not going with you, and ask your mother to accompany you. "

"Very well, " said Micheline, in a trembling voice. "I will ask her. You are not going just yet? "

"In a moment. "

"I, too, shall leave in a moment. "

The young wife did not want to lose one detail of the horrible comedy being played under her very eyes. She remained to learn, unawares, the reason for which Jeanne kept her husband.

Not thinking that he was watched, Serge had gone across to Jeanne, and affecting a smile, inquired:

"What is the matter? "

"Serious news. " And she explained that she must speak to her lover that evening.

"Where? " Serge asked, with astonishment.

"Here, " answered Jeanne.

"But your husband? " the Prince said.

"Is leaving in an hour. Our guests will not remain late. Go to the garden, and wait in the pavilion. The door of the back stairs leading to my dressing-room will be open. When everybody has gone, come up. "

"Take care; we are observed, " said Serge, uneasily.

And they began to laugh with affectation and talked aloud about frivolous things, as if nothing serious were occupying their thoughts. Cayrol had come back again. He went up to Madame Desvarennes, who was talking with her daughter, and, full of business, thoughtlessly said:

"I will telegraph you as soon as I reach London. "

"Are you going away? " inquired Micheline, a light dawning on her mind.

"Yes, " said Cayrol; "I have an important matter to settle. "

"And when do you start? " continued Micheline, in such a changed voice that her mother was frightened.

"In a moment, " answered the banker. "Allow me to leave you. I have several orders to give. "

And leaving the boudoir, he regained the little drawing-room.

Micheline, with clinched hands and fixed gaze, was saying to herself:

"She will be alone to-night, and has asked him to come to her. He told me an untruth about his having to go to the club. He is going to see her! "

And passing her hand across her brow, as if to drive away an unpleasant thought, the young wife remained silent, dismayed and crushed.

"Micheline, what is the matter with you? " asked Madame Desvarennes, seizing her daughter's hand, which was icy cold.

"Nothing, " stammered Micheline.

"You are ill, I see. Come, let us go home. Come and kiss Jeanne—"

"I! " cried Micheline, with horror, instinctively recoiling as if dreading some impure contact.

Madame Desvarennes became suddenly cold and calm. She foresaw a terrible revelation, and observing her daughter narrowly, said:

"Why do you cry out when I speak of your kissing Jeanne? Whatever is the matter? "

Micheline grasped her mother's arm, and pointed to Serge and Jeanne, who were in the little drawing-room, laughing and talking, surrounded by a group of people, yet alone.

"Look at them! " she cried.

"What do you mean? " exclaimed the mother in agony. She read the truth in her daughter's eyes.

"You know—"she began.

"That he is her lover, " cried Micheline, interrupting her. "Don't you see that I am dying through it? " she added, sobbing bitterly and falling into her mother's arms.

The mistress carried her as if she had been a child into Cayrol's private office, and shut the door. Then, kneeling beside the couch on which Micheline was stretched, she gave vent to her grief. She begged her daughter to speak to her, and warmed her hands with kisses; then, seeing her still cold and motionless, she was frightened, and wanted to call for help.

"No; be quiet! " murmured Micheline, recovering. "Let no one know. I ought to have held my peace; but I have suffered so much I could not help myself.

"My life is blasted, you see. Take me away; save me from this infamy! Jeanne, my sister, and Serge. Oh! make me forget it! For pity's sake, mamma, you who are so strong, you who have always done what you wished, take from my heart all the pain that is there! "

Madame Desvarennes, overcome by such a load of grief, lost command of herself, and, quite brokenhearted, began to cry and moan.

"O God! Micheline, my poor child! you were suffering so and did not tell me. Oh! I knew you no longer trusted your old mother. And I stupidly did not guess it! I said to myself, at least she knows nothing about it, and sacrificed everything to keep the knowledge of their wrong-doing from you. Don't cry any more, darling, you will break my heart. I, who would have given up everything in the world to see you happy! Oh, I have loved you too much! How I am punished! "

"It is I who am punished, " said Micheline, sobbing, "for not obeying you. Ah! children ought always to heed their mother. She divines the danger. Is it not too horrible, mamma? I, who have sacrificed everything for him, to think that he does not love me, and never will love me! What will my life be without confidence, hope, or affection? I am too unhappy. It would be better to die! "

"Die! you! " cried her mother, whose eyes, wet with tears, dried in a moment, as if by an inward fire. "Die! Come, don't talk such nonsense! Because a man treats you with scorn and betrays you? Are men worth dying for? No, you shall live, my darling, with your old mother. You shall have a deed of separation from your husband. "

"And he will be free, " exclaimed Micheline, angrily. "He will go on loving her! Oh! I cannot bear that thought. Do you know, what I am going to tell you seems awful. I love him so much, that I would rather see him dead than unfaithful. "

Madame Desvarennes was struck, and remained silent. Serge dead! That idea had already occurred to her as a dream of deliverance. It came upon her peremptorily, violently, irresistibly. She repelled it with an effort.

"I can never think of him but as vile and odious, " continued Micheline. "Every day his sin will seem more dastardly and his hypocrisy more base. There, a little while ago, he was smiling; and do you know why? Because Cayrol is going away, and during his absence Serge will return here tonight. "

"Who told you? "

"I read it in his joyful looks. I love him. He cannot hide anything from me. A traitor to me, and a traitor toward his friend, that is the man whom—I am ashamed to own it—I love! "

"Compose yourself! Someone is coming, " said Madame Desvarennes, and at the same time the door opened and Jeanne appeared, followed by Marechal, who was anxious at their disappearance.

"Is Micheline ill? " inquired Madame Cayrol, coming forward.

"No; it is nothing. Just a little fatigue, " said Madame Desvarennes. "Marechal, give my daughter your arm, and take her to her carriage. I shall be down in a minute. "

And holding Jeanne by the hand to prevent her following Micheline, she added:

"Stay; I have something to say to you. "

Jeanne looked surprised. Madame Desvarennes was silent for a moment. She was thinking about Serge coming there that night. She had only to say one word to Cayrol to prevent his going away. The life of this wretch was entirely in her hands then! But Jeanne! Was she going to ruin her? Had she the right thus to destroy one who had struggled and had defended herself? Would it be just? Jeanne had been led on against her will. She must question her. If the poor girl were suffering, if she repented, she must spare her.

Madame Desvarennes, having thus made up her mind, turned toward Jeanne who was waiting.

"It is a long time since I have seen you, my dear, and I find you happy and smiling. It is the first time since your marriage that you have seemed so happy. "

Jeanne looked at the mistress without answering. In these words she detected irony.

"You have found peace, " continued Madame Desvarennes, looking steadfastly at Jeanne with her piercing eyes. "You see, my dear, when you have a clear conscience—for you have nothing to reproach yourself with? "

Jeanne saw in this sentence a question and not an affirmation. She answered, boldly:

"Nothing! "

"You know that I love you, and would be most lenient, " continued Madame Desvarennes, sweetly, "and that you might safely confide in me! "

"I have nothing to fear, having nothing to tell, " said Jeanne.

"Nothing? " repeated the mistress, with emphasis.

"Nothing, " affirmed Jeanne.

Madame Desvarennes once more looked at her adopted daughter as if she would read her very soul. She found her quite calm.

"Very well, then! " said she, hastily walking toward the door.

"Are you going already? " asked Jeanne, offering her brow to Madame Desvarennes's lips.

"Yes, good-by! " said the latter, with an icy kiss.

Jeanne, without again turning round, went into the drawing-room. At the same moment, Cayrol, in a travelling-coat, entered the office, followed by Pierre.

"Here I am, quite ready, " said the banker to Madame Desvarennes. "Have you any new suggestion to make to me, or anything else to say? "

"Yes, " replied Madame Desvarennes, in a stern voice which made Cayrol start.

"Then make haste. I have only a moment to spare, and you know the train waits for no one. "

"You will not go! "

Cayrol, in amazement, answered:

"Do you mean it? Your interests are at stake yonder. "

"Your honor is in danger here, " cried the mistress, vehemently.

"My honor! " repeated Cayrol, starting back. "Madame, do you know what you are saying? "

"Ay! " answered Madame Desvarennes. "And do you remember what I promised you? I undertook to warn you, myself, if ever the day came when you would be threatened. "

"Well? " questioned Cayrol, turning quite livid.

"Well! I keep my promise. If you wish to know who your rival is, come home to-night. "

Some inaudible words rattled in Cayrol's throat.

"A rival! in my house! Can Jeanne be guilty? Do you know, if it is true I will kill them both! "

"Deal with them as your conscience dictates, " said Madame Desvarennes. "I have acted according to mine. "

Pierre, hitherto dumb with horror at the scene of which he had been a witness, shook off his stupor, and going up to Madame Desvarennes, said:

"Madame, do you know that what you have just done is frightful! "

"How? That man will be acting within his rights the same as I am. They are seeking to take away his wife, and they are killing my daughter, and dishonoring me! We are defending ourselves! Woe to those who are guilty of the crime! "

Cayrol had fallen, as if thunderstruck, on a chair, with haggard eyes; his voice was gone, and he looked the image of despair. Madame Desvarennes's words came back to him like the refrain of a hated song. To himself he kept repeating, without being able to chase away the one haunting thought: "Her lover, to-night, at your house! " He felt as if he were going mad. He was afraid he should not have time to wreak his vengeance. He made a terrible effort, and, moaning with grief, he arose.

"Take care! " said Pierre. "Here's your wife. "

Cayrol eyed Jeanne, who was approaching. Burning tears came to his eyes. He murmured:

"She, with a look so pure, and a face so calm! Is it possible? "

He nodded a farewell to Pierre and Madame Desvarennes, who were leaving, and recovering himself, advanced to meet Jeanne.

"Are you off? " she inquired. "You know you have no time to lose! "

Cayrol shuddered. She seemed anxious to get rid of him.

"I have still a few minutes to spend with you, " he said, with emotion. "You see, Jeanne, I am sad at going away alone. It is the first time I have left you. In a moment our guests will be gone—I beg of you, come with me! "

Jeanne smiled. "But you see, dear, I am in evening dress. "

"The night of our marriage I brought you away from Cernay like that. Wrap yourself up in your furs, and come! Give me this proof of affection. I deserve it. I am not a bad man—and I love you so! "

Jeanne frowned. This pressing vexed her.

"This is childish, " she said. "You will return the day after tomorrow, and I am tired. Have some pity for me. "

"You refuse? " asked Cayrol, becoming gloomy and serious.

Jeanne touched his face slightly with her white hand.

"Come! Don't leave me in a temper! You won't miss me much, you will sleep all the way. Good-by! "

Cayrol kissed her; in a choking voice, he said:

"Good-by! "

And he left her.

Jeanne's face brightened, as she stood listening for a moment and heard the carriage which contained her husband rolling away. Uttering a sigh of relief, she murmured:

"At last! "

CHAPTER XX

THE CRISIS

Jeanne had just taken off her ball-dress to put on a dressing-gown of Oriental cloth richly embroidered with silk flowers. Leaning her elbows on the mantelpiece, and breathing heavily, she was waiting. Her maid came in, bringing a second lamp. The additional light displayed the rich warm hangings of ruby plush embroidered in dull gold. The bed seemed one mass of lace.

"Has everybody gone? " asked Jeanne, pretending to yawn.

"Messieurs Le Brede and Du Tremblay, the last guests, are just putting on their overcoats, " answered the maid. "But Monsieur Pierre Delarue has come back, and is asking whether Madame will speak with him for a moment. "

"Monsieur Delarue? " repeated Jeanne, with astonishment.

"He says he has something important to say to Madame. "

"Where is he? " asked Jeanne.

"There, in the gallery. The lights were being put out in the drawing-room. "

"Well, show him in. "

The maid went out. Jeanne, much puzzled, asked herself, what could have brought Pierre back? It must certainly be something very important. She had always felt somewhat awed in Pierre's presence. At that moment the idea of being face to face with the young man was most distressing to her.

A curtain was lifted and Pierre appeared. He remained silent and confused at the entrance of the room, his courage had deserted him.

"Well, " said Jeanne, with assumed stiffness, "whatever is the matter, my friend? "

"The matter is, my dear Jeanne, " began Pierre, "that—"

But the explanation did not seem so very easy to give, for he stopped and could not go on.

"That? " repeated Madame Cayrol.

"I beg your pardon, " resumed Pierre. "I am greatly embarrassed. In coming here I obeyed a sudden impulse. I did not think of the manner in which I should tell you what I have to say, and I see that I shall have to run a great risk of offending you. "

Jeanne assumed a haughty air.

"Well, but, my dear friend, if what you have to say is so difficult, don't say it. "

"Impossible! " retorted Pierre. "My silence would cause irreparable mischief. In mercy, Jeanne, make my task easier! Meet me half way! You have projects for to-night which are known. Danger threatens you. Take care! "

Jeanne shuddered. But controlling herself, she answered, laughing nervously:

"What rubbish are you talking about? I am at home, surrounded by my servants, and I have nothing to fear. I beg of you to believe me. "

"You deny it! " exclaimed Pierre. "I expected as much. But you are only taking useless trouble. Come, Jeanne, I am the friend of your childhood; you have no reason to fear aught from me. I am only trying to be of use to you. You must know that, by my coming here, I know all. Jeanne, listen to me! "

"Are you mad? " interrupted the young woman, proudly, "or are you taking part in some absurd joke? "

"I am in my right mind, unfortunately for you! " said Pierre, roughly, seeing that Jeanne refused to believe him. "And there is no joke in the matter. Everything is true, serious and terrible! Since you compel me to say things which may be unpalatable, they must out. Prince Panine is in your house, or he soon will be. Your husband, whom you think far away, is within call, perhaps, and will come and take you unawares. Is not that a serious matter? "

A frown overspread her face, and in an ungovernable rage she stepped forward, determined not to give in, and exclaimed:

"Go away! or I shall call for assistance! "

"Don't call, it would look bad! " resumed Pierre, calmly. "On the contrary, let the servants get out of the way, and get the Prince to go if he be here, or if he has not yet arrived, prevent his coming in. So long as I remain here you will dissimulate your fear and will not take any precautions. I will leave you, then. Adieu, Jeanne! Believe that I wished to render you a service, and be sure that when I have crossed the threshold of this door I shall have forgotten everything that I may have said. "

Pierre bowed, and, lifting the heavy curtain which hid the door leading to the gallery, went out.

He had hardly gone when the opposite door opened, and Serge entered the room. The young woman rushed into his arms and whispered into his ear, with trembling lips:

"Serge, we are lost! "

"I was there, " answered Panine. "I heard all. "

"What shall we do? " cried Jeanne, terrified.

"Go away at once. To remain here a moment longer is an imprudence. "

"And I, if I remain, what shall I say to Cayrol when he comes? "

"Your husband! " said Serge, bitterly. "He loves you, he will forgive you. "

"I know; but then we two shall be separated for ever. Is that what you desire? "

"And what can I do? " cried Serge, in despair. "Everything around me is giving way! Fortune, which has been my one aim in life, is escaping from me. The family which I have scorned is forsaking me. The friendship which I have betrayed overwhelms me. There is nothing left to me. "

"And my love, my devotion? " exclaimed Jeanne, passionately. "Do you think that I will leave you? We must go away. I asked you long ago. You resisted; the moment has now come. Be easy! Madame Desvarennes will pay and save your name. In exchange you will give her back her daughter. You don't care about her, because you love me. I am your real wife; she who ought to share your life. Well, I take back my rights. I pay for them with my honor. I break all ties which could hold me back. I am yours, Serge! Our sin and misfortune will bind us more closely than any laws could. "

"Think, that with me you will have to endure poverty, and, perhaps, misery, " said the Prince, moved by the young woman's infatuation.

"My love will make you forget everything! "

"You will not feel regret or remorse? "

"Never, so long as you love me. "

"Come, then, " said the Prince, taking Jeanne in his arms. "And if life is too hard—"

"Well, " added Jeanne, finishing the sentence with sparkling eyes, "we will seek refuge together in death! Come! "

Serge bolted the door, through which Pierre had passed, and which alone communicated with the other apartments. Then, taking his mistress by the hand, he went with her into the dressing-room. Jeanne threw a dark cloak round her shoulders, put a hat on her head, and without taking either money, jewels, lace, or, in fact, anything that she had received from Cayrol, they went down the little back stairs.

It was very dark. Jeanne did not take a light, as she did not care to attract attention, so they had to feel every step of the way as quietly as possible, striving not to make the least noise, holding their breath, and with beating hearts. When they reached the bottom of the stairs, Jeanne stretched out her hand, and sought the handle of the door which opened into the courtyard. She turned it, but the door would not open. She pushed, but it did not give way. Jeanne uttered a low groan. Serge shook it vigorously, but it would not open.

"It has been fastened on the outside, " he whispered.

"Fastened? " murmured Jeanne, seized with fear. "Fastened, and by whom? "

Serge did not answer. The idea that Cayrol had done it came to his mind at once. The husband lying in wait, had seen him enter, and to prevent his escaping from his vengeance had cut off all means of retreating.

Silently, they went upstairs again, into the room through the dressing- room. Jeanne took off her bonnet and cloak, and sank into an armchair.

"I must get away! " said Serge, with suppressed rage; and he walked toward the door of the gallery.

"No! don't open that, " cried Jeanne, excitedly.

And with a frightened look, she added:

"What if he were behind the door? "

At the same moment, as if Jeanne's voice had indeed evoked Cayrol, a heavy step was heard approaching along the gallery, a hand tried to open the bolted door. Serge and Jeanne remained motionless, waiting.

"Jeanne! " called the voice of Cayrol from the outside, sounding mournfully in the silence, "Jeanne, open! "

And with his fist he knocked imperatively on the woodwork.

"I know you are there! Open, I say! " he cried, with increasing rage. "If you don't open the door, I'll—"

"Go! I beseech you! " whispered Jeanne, in Panine's ear. "Go downstairs again, and break open the door. You won't find any one there now. "

"Perhaps he has stationed some one there, " answered Serge. "Besides, I won't leave you here alone exposed to his violence. "

"You are not alone. I can hear you talking! " said Cayrol, beside himself. "I shall break open this door! "

The husband made a tremendous effort. Under the pressure of his heavy weight the lock gave way. With a bound he was in the middle of the room. Jeanne threw herself before him; she no longer trembled. Cayrol took another step and fixed his glaring eyes on the man whom he sought, uttering a fearful oath.

"Serge! " cried he. "I might have guessed it. It is not only money of which you are robbing me, you villain! "

Panine turned horribly pale, and advanced toward Cayrol, despite Jeanne, who was clinging to him.

"Don't insult me; it is superfluous, " said he. "My life belongs to you; you can take it. I shall be at your service whenever you please. "

Cayrol burst into a fearful laugh.

"Ah! a duel! Come! Am I a gentleman? I am a plebeian! a rustic! a cowherd! you know that! I have you now! I am going to smash you! "

He looked round the room as if seeking a weapon, and caught sight of the heavy fire-dogs. He caught up one with a cry of triumph, and, brandishing it like a club, rushed at Serge.

More rapid than he, Jeanne threw herself before her lover. She stretched out her arms, and with a sharp voice, and the look of a she-wolf defending her cubs,

"Keep behind me, " said she to Serge; "he loves me and will not dare to strike! "

Cayrol had stopped. At these words he uttered a loud cry: "wretched woman! You first, then! "

Raising his weapon, he was about to strike, when his eyes met Jeanne's. The young woman was smiling, happy to die for her lover. Her pale face beamed from out her black hair with weird beauty. Cayrol trembled. That look which he had loved, would he never see it again? That rosy mouth, whose smile he cherished, would it be hushed in death? A thousand thoughts of happy days came to his mind. His arm fell. A bitter flood rushed from his heart to his eyes; the iron dropped heavily from his hand on to the floor, and the poor man, overcome, sobbing, and ashamed of his weakness, fell senseless on a couch.

Jeanne did not utter a word. By a sign she showed Serge the door, which was open, and with a swollen heart she leaned on the mantelpiece, waiting for the unfortunate man, from whom she had received such a deep and sad proof of love, to come back to life.

Serge had disappeared.

CHAPTER XXI

"WHEN ROGUES FALL OUT"

The night seemed long to Madame Desvarennes. Agitated and feverish, she listened through the silence, expecting every moment to hear some fearful news. In fancy she saw Cayrol entering his wife's room like a madman, unawares. She seemed to hear a cry of rage, answered by a sigh of terror; then a double shot resounded, the room filled with smoke, and, struck down in their guilty love, Serge and Jeanne rolled in death, interlaced in each other's arms, like Paolo and Francesca de Rimini, those sad lovers of whom Dante tells us.

Hour after hour passed; not a sound disturbed the mansion. The Prince had not come in. Madame Desvarennes, unable to lie in bed, arose, and now and again, to pass the time, stole on tiptoe to her daughter's room. Micheline, thoroughly exhausted with fatigue and emotion, had fallen asleep on her pillow, which was wet with tears.

Bending over her, by the light of the lamp, the mistress gazed at Micheline's pale face, and a sigh rose to her lips.

"She is still young, " she thought; "she may begin life afresh. The remembrance of these sad days will be wiped out, and I shall see her revive and smile again. That wretch was nearly the death of her. "

And the image of Serge and Jeanne stretched beside each other in the room full of smoke came before her eyes again. She shook her head to chase the importunate vision away, and noiselessly regained her own apartment.

The day dawned pale and bleak. Madame Desvarennes opened her window and cooled her burning brow in the fresh morning air. The birds were awake, and were singing on the trees in the garden.

Little by little, the distant sound of wheels rolling by was heard. The city was awakening from its sleep.

Madame Desvarennes rang and asked for Marechal. The secretary appeared instantly. He, too, had shared the anxieties and fears of the mistress, and had risen early. Madame Desvarennes greeted him with a grateful smile. She felt that she was really loved by this good fellow, who understood her so thoroughly. She begged him to go to Cayrol's, and gain some information, without giving him further details, and she waited, walking up and down the room to calm the fever of her mind.

On leaving the house in the Rue Taitbout, Serge felt bewildered, not daring to go home, and unable to decide on any plan; yet feeling that it was necessary to fix on something without delay, he reached the club. The walk did him good, and restored his physical equilibrium. He was thankful to be alive after such a narrow escape. He went upstairs with a comparatively light step, and tossed his overcoat to a very sleepy footman who had risen to receive him. He went into the card-room. Baccarat was just finishing. It was three o'clock in the morning. The appearance of the Prince lent the game a little fresh animation. Serge plunged into it as if it were a battle. Luck was on his side. In a short time he cleared the bank: a thousand louis. One by one the players retired. Panine, left alone, threw himself on a couch and slept for a few hours, but it was not a refreshing sleep. On the contrary, it made him feel more tired.

The day servants disturbed him when they came in to sweep the rooms and open the windows. He went into the lavatory, and there bathed his face. When his ablutions were over he wrote a note to Jeanne, saying that he had reflected, and could not possibly let her go away with him. He implored her to do all in her power to forget him. He gave this letter to one of the messengers, and told him to give it into the hands of Madame Cayrol's maid, and to none other.

The care of a woman and the worry of another household seemed unbearable to him. Besides, what could he do with Jeanne? The presence of his mistress would prevent his being able to go back to Micheline. And now he felt that his only hope of safety was in Micheline's love for him.

But first of all he must go and see if Herzog had returned, and ascertain the real facts of the position in regard to the Universal Credit Company.

Herzog occupied a little house on the Boulevard Haussmann, which he had hired furnished from some Americans. The loud luxury of the Yankees had not frightened him. On the contrary, he held that the gay colors of the furniture and the glitter of the gilded cornices were bound to have a fascination for prospective shareholders.

Suzanne had reserved a little corner for herself, modestly hung with muslin and furnished with simple taste, which was a great contrast to the loud appearance of the other part of the house.

On arriving, Serge found a stableman washing a victoria. Herzog had returned. The Prince quietly went up the steps, and had himself announced.

The financier was sitting in his study by the window, looking through the newspapers. When Serge entered he rose. The two men stood facing each other for a moment. The Prince was the first to speak.

"How is it that you have kept me without news during your absence? " asked he, harshly.

"Because, " replied Herzog, calmly, "the only news I had was not good news. "

"At least I should have known it. "

"Would the result of the operation have been different? "

"You have led me like a child in this affair, " Serge continued, becoming animated. "I did not know where I was going. You made me promises, how have you kept them? "

"As I was able, " quietly answered Herzog. "Play has its chances. One seeks Austerlitz and finds Waterloo. "

"But, " cried the Prince, angrily, "the shares which you sold ought not to have gone out of your hands. "

"You believed that? " retorted the financier, ironically. "If they ought not to have gone out of my hands it was hardly worth while putting them into them. "

"In short, " said Panine, eager to find some responsible party on whom he could pour out all the bitterness of his misfortune, "you took a mean advantage of me. "

"Good! I expected you to say that! " returned Herzog, smiling. "If the business had succeeded, you would have accepted your share of the spoil without any scruples, and would have felt ready to crown me. It has failed; you are trying to get out of the responsibility, and are on the point of treating me as if I were a swindler. Still, the affair would not have been more honest in the first instance than in the second, but success embellishes everything. "

Serge looked hard at Herzog.

"What is there to prove, " replied he, "that this speculation, which brings ruin and loss to me, does not enrich you? "

"Ungrateful fellow! " observed the financier, ironically, "you suspect me! "

"Of having robbed me! " cried Serge, in a rage. "Why not? "

Herzog, for a moment, lost his temper and turned red in the face. He seized Panine violently by the arm, and said:

"Gently, Prince; whatever insults you heap upon me must be shared by you. You are my partner. "

"Scoundrel! " yelled Panine, exasperated at being held by Herzog.

"Personalities, " said the financier, in a jesting tone. "Then I take my leave! "

And loosing his hold of the Prince, he went toward the door.

Serge sprang after him, exclaiming:

"You shall not leave this room until you have given me the means of rectifying this disaster. "

"Then let us talk sensibly, as boon companions, " said Herzog. "I know of a marvellous move by which we can get out of the difficulty. Let us boldly call a general meeting. I will explain the thing, and amaze everybody. We shall get a vote of confidence for the past, with funds for the future. We shall be as white as snow, and the game is played. Are you in with me? "

"Enough, " replied the Prince, intensely disgusted. "It does not suit me to do a yet more shameful thing in order to get out of this trouble. It is no use arguing further; we are lost. "

"Only the weak allow themselves to be lost! " exclaimed the financier. "The strong defend themselves. You may give in if you like; I won't. Three times have I been ruined and three times have I risen again. My head is good! I am down now. I shall rise again, and when I am well off, and have a few millions to spare, I will settle old debts. Everybody will be astonished because they won't expect it, and I shall be more thought of than if I had paid up at the time. "

"And if you are not allowed to go free? " asked Serge. "What if they arrest you? "

"I shall be in Aix-la-Chapelle to-night, " said Herzog. "From there I shall treat with the shareholders of the Universal Credit. People judge things better at a distance. Are you coming with me? "

"No, " replied Serge, in a low voice.

"You are wrong. Fortune is capricious, and in six months we may be richer than we ever have been. But as you have decided, let me give you a piece of advice which will be worth the money you have lost. Confess all to your wife; she can get you out of this difficulty. "

The financier held out a hand to Serge which he did not take.

"Ah! pride! " murmured Herzog. "After all it is your right—It is you who pay! "

Without answering a word the Prince went out.

At that same hour, Madame Desvarennes, tired by long waiting, was pacing up and down her little drawing-room. A door opened and Marechal, the long-looked for messenger, appeared. He had been to Cayrol's, but could not see him. The banker, who had shut himself up in his private office where he had worked all night, had given orders that no one should interrupt him. And as Madame Desvarennes seemed to have a question on her lips which she dared not utter, Marechal added that nothing unusual seemed to have happened at the house.

But as the mistress was thanking her secretary, the great gate swung on its hinges, and a carriage rolled into the courtyard. Marechal flew to the window, and uttered one word,

"Cayrol! "

Madame Desvarennes motioned to him to leave her, and the banker appeared on the threshold.

At a glance the mistress saw the ravages which the terrible night he had passed through had caused. Yesterday, the banker was rosy, firm, and upright as an oak, now he was bent, and withered like an old man. His hair had become gray about the temples, as if scorched by his burning thoughts. He was only the shadow of himself.

Madame Desvarennes advanced toward him, and in one word asked a world of questions.

"Well? " she said.

Cayrol, gloomy and fierce, raised his eyes to the mistress, and answered:

"Nothing! "

"Did he not come? "

"Yes, he came. But I had not the necessary energy to kill him. I thought it was an easier matter to become a murderer. And you thought so too, eh? "

"Cayrol! " cried Madame Desvarennes, shuddering, and troubled to find that she had been so easily understood by him whom she had armed on her behalf.

"The opportunity was a rare one, though, " continued Cayrol, getting excited. "Fancy; I found them together under my own roof. The law allowed me, if not the actual right to kill them, at least an excuse if I did so. Well, at the decisive moment, when I ought to have struck the blow, my heart failed me. He lives, and Jeanne loves him. "

There was a pause.

"What are you going to do? "

"Get rid of him in another way, " answered Cayrol. "I had only two ways of killing him. One was to catch him in my own house, the other to call him out. My will failed me in the one case; my want of skill would fail me in the other. I will not fight Serge. Not because I fear death, for my life is blighted, and I don't value it; but if I were dead, Jeanne would belong to him, and I could not bear the thought of that even in death. I must separate them forever. "

"And how? "

"By forcing him to disappear. "

"And if he refuse? "

Cayrol shook his head menacingly, and exclaimed:

"I defy him! If he resist, I will bring him before the assizes! "

"You? " said Madame Desvarennes, going nearer to Cayrol.

"Yes, I! " answered the banker, with energy.

"Wretched man! And my daughter? " cried the mistress. "Think well what you are saying! You would disgrace me and mine. "

"Am I not dishonored myself? " asked Cayrol. "Your son-in-law is a robber, who has defiled my home and robbed my safe. "

"An honest man does not seek to revenge himself after the manner you suggest, " said the mistress, gravely.

"An honest man defends himself as he can. I am not a knight. I am only a financier. Money is my weapon. The Prince has stolen from me. I will have him sentenced as a thief. "

Madame Desvarennes frowned.

"Make out your account. I will pay it. "

"Will you also pay me for my lost happiness? " cried the banker, exasperated. "Should I not rather have chosen to be ruined than be betrayed as I am? You can never repair the wrong he has done me. And then I am suffering so, I must have my revenge! "

"Ah! fool that you are, " replied Madame Desvarennes. "The guilty will not feel your blows, but the innocent. When my daughter and I are in despair will you be less unhappy! Oh! Cayrol, take heed that you lose not in dignity what you gain in revenge. The less one is respected by others the more one must respect one's self. Contempt and silence elevate the victim, while rage and hatred make him descend to the level of those who have outraged him. "

"Let people judge me as they please. I care only for myself! I am a vulgar soul, and have a low mind—anything you like. But the idea that that woman belongs to another drives me mad. I ought to hate her, but, notwithstanding everything, I cannot live without her. If she will come back to me I will forgive her. It is ignoble! I feel it, but it is too strong for me. I adore her! "

Before that blind love Madame Desvarennes shuddered. She thought of Micheline who loved Serge as Cayrol loved Jeanne.

"Suppose she chooses to go away with Serge, " said the mistress to herself. In a moment she saw the house abandoned, Micheline and Serge in foreign lands, and she alone in the midst of her overthrown happiness, dying of sadness and regrets. She made a last effort to move Cayrol.

"Come, must I appeal in vain? Can you forget that I was a sure and devoted friend to you, and that you owe your fortune to me? You are a good man and will not forget the past. You have been outraged and have the right of seeking revenge, but think that in carrying it out you will hurt two women who have never done you any harm. Be generous! Be just! Spare us! "

Cayrol remained silent; his face did not relax. After a moment he said:

"You see how low I have fallen, by not yielding at once to your supplications! Friendship, gratitude, generosity, all the good feelings I had, have been consumed by this execrable love. There is nothing left but love for her. For her, I forget everything. I degrade and debase myself. And what is worse than all, is that I know all this and yet I cannot help myself. "

"Miserable man! " murmured the mistress.

"Oh! most miserable, " sobbed Cayrol, falling into an armchair.

Madame Desvarennes approached him, and quietly placed her hand on his shoulder.

"Cayrol, you are weeping? Then, forgive. "

The banker arose and, with lowering brow, said:

"No! my resolution is irrevocable. I wish to place a world between Jeanne and Serge. If he has not gone away by tonight my complaint will be lodged in the courts of justice. "

Madame Desvarennes no longer persisted. She saw that the husband's heart was permanently closed.

"It is well. I thank you for having warned me. You might have taken action without doing so. Good-by, Cayrol. I leave your conscience to judge between you and me. "

The banker bowed, and murmured:

"Good-by! "

And with a heavy step, almost tottering, he went out.

The sun had risen, and lit up the trees in the garden. Nature seemed to be making holiday. The flowers perfumed the air, and in the deep blue sky swallows were flying to and fro. This earthly joy exasperated Madame Desvarennes. She would have liked the world to be in mourning. She closed the window hastily, and remained lost in her own reflections.

So everything was over! The great prosperity, the honor of the house, everything was foundering in a moment. Even her daughter might escape from her, and follow the infamous husband whom she adored in spite of his faults—perhaps because of his very faults— and might drag on a weary existence in a strange land, which would terminate in death.

For that sweet and delicate child could not live without material comforts and mental ease, and her husband was doomed to go on from bad to worse, and would drag her down with him! The mistress pictured her daughter, that child whom she had brought up with the tenderest care, dying on a pallet, and the husband, odious to the last, refusing her admission to the room where Micheline was in agony.

A fearful feeling of anger overcame her. Her motherly love gained the mastery, and in the silence of the room she roared out these words:

"That shall not be! "

The opening of the door recalled her to her senses, and she rose. It was Marechal, greatly agitated. After Cayrol's arrival, not knowing what to do, he had gone to the Universal Credit Company, and there, to his astonishment, had found the offices closed. He had heard from the porter, one of those superb personages dressed in blue and red cloth, who were so important in the eyes of the shareholders, that the evening before, owing to the complaint of a director, the police had entered the offices, and taken the books away, and that the official seal had been placed on the doors. Marechal, much alarmed, had hastened back to Madame Desvarennes to apprise her of the fact. It was evidently necessary to take immediate steps to meet this new complication. Was this indeed the beginning of legal proceedings? And if so how would the Prince come out of it?

Madame Desvarennes listened to Marechal, without uttering a word. Events were hurrying on even quicker than she had dreaded. The fears of the interested shareholders outran even the hatred of Cayrol. What would the judges call Herzog's underhand dealings? Would it be embezzlement? Or forgery? Would they come and arrest the Prince at her house? The house of Desvarennes, which had never received a visit from a sheriff's officer, was it to be disgraced now by the presence of the police?

The mistress, in that fatal hour, became herself again. The strong-minded woman of old reappeared. Marechal was more alarmed at this sudden vigor than he had been at her late depression. When he saw Madame Desvarennes going toward the door, he made an effort to detain her.

"Where are you going, Madame? " he inquired, with anxiety.

The mistress gave him a look that terrified him, and answered:

"I am going to square accounts with the Prince. "

And, passing through the door leading to the little staircase, Madame Desvarennes went up to her son-in-law's rooms.

CHAPTER XXII

THE MOTHER'S REVENGE

On leaving Herzog, Serge had turned his steps toward the Rue Saint-Dominique. He had delayed the moment of going home as long as possible, but the streets were beginning to be crowded. He might meet some people of his acquaintance. He resolved to face what ever reception was awaiting him on the way, he was planning what course he should adopt to bring about a reconciliation with his redoubtable mother-in-law. He was no longer proud, but felt quite broken down. Only Madame Desvarennes could put him on his feet again; and, as cowardly in trouble as he had been insolent in prosperity, he accepted beforehand all that she might impose upon him; all, provided that she would cover him with her protection.

He was frightened, not knowing how deep Herzog had led him in the mire. His moral sense had disappeared, but he had a vague instinct of the danger he had incurred. The financier's last words came to his mind: "Confess all to your wife; she can get you out of this difficulty! " He understood the meaning of them, and resolved to follow the advice. Micheline loved him. In appealing to her heart, deeply wounded as it was, he would have in her an ally, and he had long known that Madame Desvarennes could not oppose her daughter in anything.

He entered the house through the back garden gate, and regained his room without making the slightest noise. He dreaded meeting Madame Desvarennes before seeing Micheline. First he changed his attire; he had walked about Paris in evening clothes. Looking in the glass he was surprised at the alteration in his features. Was his beauty going too? What would become of him if he failed to please. And, like an actor who is about to play an important part, he paid great attention to the making up of his face. He wished once more to captivate his wife, as his safety depended on the impression he was about to make on her. At last, satisfied with himself, he tried to look smiling, and went to his wife's room.

Micheline was up.

At the sight of Serge she could not suppress an exclamation of surprise. It was a long time since he had discontinued these familiar visits. The presence of her beloved one in that room, which had seemed so empty when he was not there, made her feel happy, and she went to him with a smile, holding out her hand. Serge drew her gently toward him and kissed her hair.

"Up, already, dear child, " said he, affectionately.

"I have scarcely slept, " answered Micheline. "I was so anxious. I sat up for you part of the night. I had left you without saying good-night. It was the first time it had occurred, and I wanted to beg your pardon. But you came in very late. "

"Micheline, it is I who am ungrateful, " interrupted Panine, making the young wife sit down beside him. "It is I who must ask you to be indulgent. "

"Serge! I beg of you! " said the young wife, taking both his hands. "All is forgotten. I would not reproach you, I love you so much! "

Micheline's face beamed with joy, and tears filled her eyes.

"You are weeping, " said Panine. "Ah! I feel the weight of my wrongs toward you. I see how deserving you are of respect and affection. I feel unworthy, and would kneel before you to say how I regret all the anxieties I have caused you, and that my only desire in the future will be to make you forget them. "

"Oh! speak on! speak on! " cried Micheline, with delight. "What happiness to hear you say such sweet words! Open your heart to me! You know I would die to please you. If you have any anxieties or annoyances confide in me. I can relieve them. Who could resist me when you are in question? "

"I have none, Micheline, " answered Serge, with the constrained manner of a man who is feigning. "Nothing but the regret of not having lived more for you. "

"Is the future not in store for us? " said the young wife, looking lovingly at him.

The Prince shook his head, saying:

"Who can answer for the future? "

Micheline came closer to her husband, not quite understanding what Serge meant, but her mind was on the alert, and in an alarmed tone, she resumed:

"What strange words you are uttering? Are we not both young? And, if you like, is there not much happiness in store for us? "

And she clung to him. Serge turned away.

"Oh, stay, " she murmured, again putting her arms round him. "You are so truly mine at this moment! "

Panine saw that the opportunity for confessing all had come. He was able to bring tears to his eyes, and went toward the window as if to hide his emotion. Micheline followed him, and, in an eager tone, continued:

"Ah! I knew you were hiding something. You are unhappy or in pain; threatened perhaps? Ah! if you love me, tell me the truth! "

"Well, yes! It is true, I am threatened. I am suffering and unhappy! But don't expect a confession from me. I should blush to make it. But, thank Heaven, if I cannot extricate myself from the difficulty in which I am placed through my own folly and imprudence—there is yet another way out of it. "

"Serge! you would kill yourself! " cried Micheline, terrified at the gesture Panine had made. "What would become of me then? But what is there that is so hard to explain? And to whom should it be said? "

"To your mother, " answered Serge, bowing his head.

"To my mother? Very well, I will go to her. Oh! don't fear anything. I can defend you, and to strike you she will first have to attack me. "

Serge put his arms round Micheline, and with a kiss, the hypocrite inspired her whom he entrusted with his safety with indomitable courage.

"Wait for me here, " added the young wife, and passing through the little drawing-room she reached the smoking-room.

He halted there a moment

She halted there a moment, out of breath and almost choked with emotion. The long expected day had arrived. Serge was coming back to her. She went on, and as she reached the door of the stair leading to her mother's rooms, she heard a light tap from without.

Greatly astonished, she opened the door, and suddenly drew back, uttering an exclamation. A woman, thickly veiled, stood before her.

At the sight of Micheline the stranger seemed inclined to turn and fly. But overcome with jealousy, the young wife seized her by the arm, dragged off her veil, and recognizing her, exclaimed:

"Jeanne! "

Madame Cayrol approached Micheline, and beseechingly stretched out her hands:

"Micheline! don't think—I come—"

"Hold your tongue! " cried Micheline. "Don't tell me any lies! I know all! You are my husband's mistress! "

Crushed by such a stroke, Jeanne hid her face in her hands and moaned:

"O God! "

"You must really be bold, " continued Micheline, in a furious tone, "to seek him here, in my house, almost in my arms! "

Jeanne drew herself up, blushing with shame and grief.

"Ah! don't think, " she said, "that love brings me here. "

"What is it then? " asked Micheline, contemptuously.

"The knowledge of inevitable and pressing danger which threatens Serge. "

"A danger! Of what kind? "

"Compromised by Herzog, he is at the mercy of my husband, who has sworn to ruin him. "

"Your husband! "

"Yes, he is his rival. If you could ruin me, would you not do it? " said Jeanne.

"You! " retorted Micheline, passionately. "Do you think I am going to worry about you? Serge is my first thought. You say you came to warn him. What must be done? "

"Without a moment's delay he must go away! "

A strange suspicion crossed Micheline's mind. She approached Jeanne, and looking earnestly at her, said:

"He must go away without delay, eh? And it is you, braving everything, without a thought of the trouble you leave behind you, who come to warn him? Ah! you mean to go with him? "

Jeanne hesitated a moment. Then, boldly and impudently, defying and almost threatening the legitimate wife:

"Well, yes, I wish to! Enough of dissimulation! I love him! " she exclaimed.

Micheline, transfigured by passion, strong, and ready for a struggle, threw herself in Jeanne's way, with arms outstretched, as if to prevent her going to Serge.

"Well! " she said; "try to take him from me! "

"Take him from you! " answered Jeanne, laughing like a mad woman. "To whom does he most belong? To the woman who was as ignorant of his love as she was of his danger; who could do nothing toward his happiness, and can do nothing for his safety? Or to the mistress who has sacrificed her honor to please him and risks her safety to save him? "

"Ah! wretch! " cried Micheline, "to invoke your infamy as a right! "

"Which of us has taken him from the other? " continued Jeanne, forgetting respect, modesty, everything. "Do you know that he loved me before he married you? Do you know that he abandoned me for you—for your money, I should say? Now, do you wish to weigh what I have suffered with what you suffer? Shall we make out a balance-sheet of our tears? Then, you will be able to tell which of us he has loved more, and to whom he really belongs. "

Micheline had listened to this furious address almost in a state of stupor, and replied, vehemently:

"What matter who triumphs if his ruin is certain. Selfish creatures that we are, instead of disputing about his love, let us unite in saving him! You say he must go away! But flight is surely an admission of guilt— humiliation and obscurity in a strange land. And that is what you advise, because you hope to share that miserable existence with him. You are urging him on to dishonor. His fate is in the hands of a man who adores you, who would sacrifice everything for you, as I would for Serge, and yet you have not thrown yourself at his feet! You have not offered your life as the price of your lover's! And you say that you love him! "

"Ah! " stammered Jeanne, distracted. "You wish me to save him for you! "

"Is that the cry of your heart? " said Micheline, with crushing disdain. "Well, see what I am ready to do. If, to remove your jealous fears, it is necessary to sacrifice myself, I swear to you that if Serge be saved, he shall be perfectly free, and I will never see him again! "

Micheline, chaste and calm, with hands raised to Heaven, seemed to grow taller and nobler. Jeanne, trembling and overpowered, looked at her rival with a painful effort, and murmured, softly:

"Would you do that? "

"I would do more! " said the lawful wife, bending before the mistress. "I ought to hate you, and I kneel at your feet and beseech you to listen to me. Do what I ask you and I will forgive you and bless you. Do not hesitate! Follow me! Let us throw ourselves at the feet of him whom you have outraged. His generosity cannot be less than ours, and to us, who sacrifice our love, he will not be able to refuse to sacrifice his vengeance. "

This greatness and goodness awaked feelings in Jeanne's heart which she thought dead. She was silent for a moment and then her breast heaved with convulsive sobs, and she fell helpless into the arms which Micheline, full of pity, held out to her.

"Forgive me, " moaned the unhappy woman. "I am conquered. Your rights are sacred, and you have just made them still more so. Keep Serge: with you he will once more become honest and happy, because, if your love is not greater than mine, it is nobler and purer. "

The two women went hand in hand to try to save the man whom they both adored.

All this time Serge remained in the little drawing-room enjoying the hope of returning peace. It was sweet to him, after the troubles he had gone through. He had not the slightest suspicion of the scene in the adjoining room between Jeanne and Micheline. The fond heroism of his wife and the self-denial of his mistress were unknown to him.

Time was passing. At least an hour had sped since Micheline left him to go to her mother, and Serge was beginning to think that the interview was very long, when a light step made him tremble. It came from the gallery. He thought it was Micheline, and opening the door, he went to meet her.

He drew back disappointed, vexed, and anxious, when he found it was Pierre. The two men had never met alone since that terrible night at Nice. Panine assumed a bold demeanor, and returned Pierre's firm look. Steadying his voice, he said:

"Ah! is it you? "

"Were you not expecting me? " answered Pierre whose harsh voice thrilled Serge.

The Prince opened his mouth to speak, but Pierre, did not give him time. In stern and provoking accents, he continued:

"I made you a promise once; have you forgotten it? I have a good memory. You are a villain, and I come to chastise you! "

"Pierre! " exclaimed the Prince, starting fiercely.

But he suddenly calmed himself, and added:

"Leave me! I will not listen to you! "

"You will have to, though! You are a source of trouble and shame to the family to which you have allied yourself, and as you have not the courage to kill yourself, I have come to help you. You must leave Paris to- night, or you will be arrested. We shall go together to Brussels and there we shall fight. If chance favors you, you will be at liberty to continue your infamies, but at any rate I shall have done my best to rid two unfortunate women of your presence. "

"You are mad! " said Serge, sneeringly.

"Don't think so! And know that I am ready for any emergency. Come; must I strike you, to give you courage? " growled Pierre, ready to suit the action to the word.

"Ah! take care! " snarled Serge, with an evil look.

And opening a drawer which was close to him, he took out a revolver.

"Thief first, then murderer! " said Pierre, with a terrible laugh. "Come, let's see you do it! "

And he was going toward the Prince when the door opened, and Madame Desvarennes came forward. Placing her hand on Pierre's shoulder, she said, in that commanding tone which few could resist:

"Go; wait for me in my room. I wish it! "

Pierre bowed, and, without answering, went out.

Serge had placed the pistol on the table and was waiting.

"We have to talk over several matters, " said Madame Desvarennes, gravely, "and you know it. "

"Yes, Madame, " answered Panine, sadly, "and, believe me, no one judges my conduct more severely than I do. "

The mistress could not help looking surprised.

"Ah! " she said, with irony, "I did not expect to find you in such a mood. You have not accustomed me to such humility and sweetness. You must be afraid, to have arrived at that stage! "

The Prince appeared not to have understood the implied insult in his mother-in-law's words. One thing struck him, which was that she evidently did not expect to find him repentant and humbled.

"Micheline must have told you, " he began.

"I have not seen my daughter, " interrupted the mistress, sharply, as if to make him understand that he must depend solely upon himself.

Ignorant that Micheline had met Jeanne on her way to her mother, and had gone to Cayrol, Serge thought he was abandoned by his only powerful ally. He saw that he was lost and that his feigned resignation was useless. Unable to control himself any longer, his face darkened with rage.

"She, too, against me! Well! I will defend myself alone! "

Turning toward Madame Desvarennes, he added:

"To begin with, what do you want with me? "

"I wish to ask you a question. We business folk when we fail, and cannot pay our way, throw blood on the blot and it disappears. You members of the nobility, when you are disgraced, how do you manage? "

"If I am not mistaken, Madame, " answered the Prince, in a light tone, "you do me the favor of asking what my intentions are for the future? I will answer you with precision. I purpose leaving to-night for Aix-la- Chapelle, where I shall join my friend Herzog. We shall begin our business again. My wife, on whose good feelings I rely, will accompany me, notwithstanding everything. "

And in these last words he put all the venom of his soul.

"My daughter will not leave me! " exclaimed Madame Desvarennes.

"Very well, then, you can accompany her, " retorted Panine. "That arrangement will suit me. Since my troubles I have learned to appreciate domestic happiness. "

"Ah! you hope to play your old games on me, " said Madame Desvarennes. "You won't get much out of me. My daughter and I with you—in the stream where you are going to sink? Never! "

"Well, then, " cried Panine, "what do you expect? "

A violent ring at the front door resounded as Madame Desvarennes was about to answer, and stopped the words on her lips. This signal, which was used only on important occasions, sounded to Madame like a funeral knell. Serge frowned, and instinctively moved back.

Marechal appeared through the half-open door with a scared face, and silently handed Madame Desvarennes a card. She glanced at it, turned pale, and said to the secretary:

"Very well, let him wait! " She threw the card on the table. Serge came forward and read:

"Delbarre, sheriff's officer. "

Haggard-looking and aghast, he turned to the mistress, as if seeking an explanation.

"Well! " she observed: "it is clear, he has come to arrest you. "

Serge rushed to a cabinet, and opening a drawer, took forth some handfuls of gold and notes, which he crammed into his pockets.

"By the back stairs I shall have time to get away. It is my last chance! Keep the man for five minutes only. "

"And if the door is guarded? " asked Madame Desvarennes.

Serge remained abject before her. He felt himself enclosed in a ring which he could not break through.

"One may be prosecuted without being condemned, " he gasped. "You will use your influence, I know, and you will get me out of this mess. I shall be grateful to you for ever, and will do anything you like! But don't leave me, it would be cowardly! "

He trembled, as he thus besought her distractedly.

"The son-in-law of Madame Desvarennes does not go before the Assize Courts even to be acquitted, " said she, with a firm voice.

"What would you have me do? " cried Serge, passionately.

Madame Desvarennes did not answer, but pointed to the revolver on the table.

"Kill myself? Ah! no; that would be giving you too much pleasure. "

And he gave the weapon a push, so that it rolled close to Madame Desvarennes.

"Ah! wretch! " cried she, giving way to her suppressed rage. "You are not even a Panine! The Panines knew how to die. "

"I have not time to act a melodrama with you, " snarled Serge. "I am going to try to save myself. "

And he took a step toward the door.

The mistress seized the revolver, and threw herself before him.

"You shall not go out! " she cried.

"Are you mad? " he exclaimed, gnashing his teeth.

"You shall not go out! " repeated the mistress, with flashing eyes.

"We shall see! "

And with a strong arm he seized Madame Desvarennes, and threw her aside.

The mistress became livid. Serge had his hand on the handle of the door. He was about to escape. Madame Desvarennes's arm was stretched forth.

A shot made the windows rattle; the weapon fell from her hand, having done its work and, amid the smoke, a body dropped heavily on the carpet, which was soon dyed with blood.

At the same moment, the door opened, and Micheline entered, holding in her hand the fatal receipt which she had just wrung from Cayrol. The young wife uttered a heartrending cry, and fell senseless on Serge's body.

Behind Micheline came the officer and Marechal. The secretary exchanged looks with the mistress, who was lifting her fainting daughter and clasping her in her arms. He understood all.

Turning toward his companion, he said:

"Alas! sir, here is a sad matter! The Prince, on hearing that you had come, took fright, although his fault was not very serious, and has shot himself. "

The officer bowed respectfully to the mistress, who was bending over Micheline.

"Please to withdraw, Madame. You have already suffered too much, " said he. "I understand your legitimate grief. If I need any information, this gentleman will give it to me. "

Madame Desvarennes arose, and, without bending under the burden, she bore away on her bosom her daughter, regained.

Lightning Source UK Ltd.
Milton Keynes UK
UKHW01065121062I
385893UK00001B/205